7 SIMPLE STEPS to STUDYING SCRIPTURE

How to Journal Your Way through the Word of God

Angella Bundz

Copyright © 2020 by Angella Bundz

www.AngellaBundz.com

All rights reserved. This book or any portion thereof may not be reproduced or used in any manner whatsoever without the express written permission of the publisher except for the use of brief quotations in a book review.

Graphics on cover and pages courtesy of Freepik.com/azerbaijan_stockers

ISBN: 978-0-578-73097-4

Printed in the United States of America.

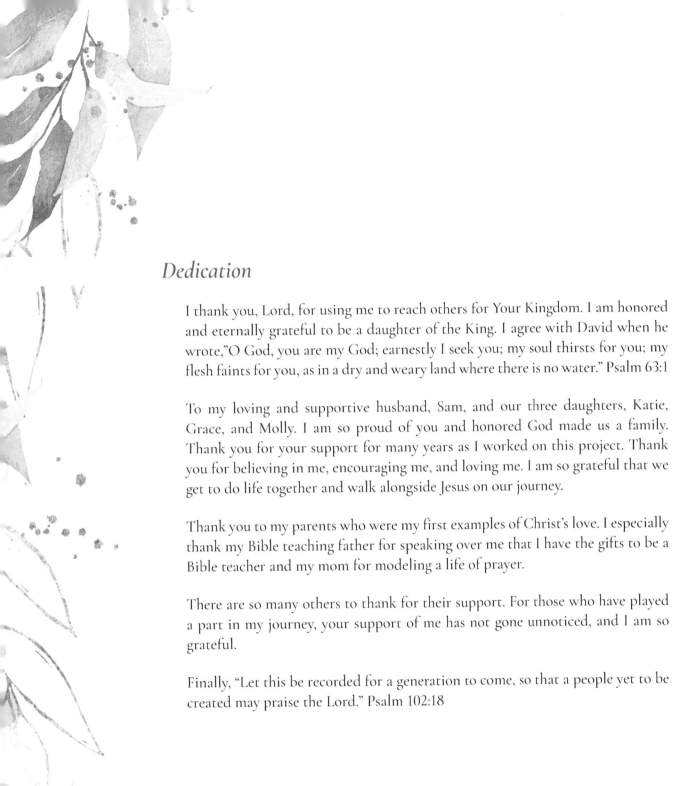

Dedication

I thank you, Lord, for using me to reach others for Your Kingdom. I am honored and eternally grateful to be a daughter of the King. I agree with David when he wrote,"O God, you are my God; earnestly I seek you; my soul thirsts for you; my flesh faints for you, as in a dry and weary land where there is no water." Psalm 63:1

To my loving and supportive husband, Sam, and our three daughters, Katie, Grace, and Molly. I am so proud of you and honored God made us a family. Thank you for your support for many years as I worked on this project. Thank you for believing in me, encouraging me, and loving me. I am so grateful that we get to do life together and walk alongside Jesus on our journey.

Thank you to my parents who were my first examples of Christ's love. I especially thank my Bible teaching father for speaking over me that I have the gifts to be a Bible teacher and my mom for modeling a life of prayer.

There are so many others to thank for their support. For those who have played a part in my journey, your support of me has not gone unnoticed, and I am so grateful.

Finally, "Let this be recorded for a generation to come, so that a people yet to be created may praise the Lord." Psalm 102:18

A Note from Angella

Welcome to *7 Simple Steps to Studying Scripture*, friend!

I am so glad that you are here! Being here means that you want to grow closer to God and understand His Word, and that's exactly why I created this guided journal. As you write on each page, my hope is that you can fall in love with God and His Word for the first time or all over again.

God's Word is powerful, and this journal will be a method for Him to speak to you in a personal way. You won't just be *informed*, but be *transformed*! I can't wait for you to discover God's love and the truths He wants to share with you!

Where it all began...

Writing this book began after my mentor, Linda Werner, suggested that I start journaling so I could see God's hand in my life. I had grown up in a Christian home and loved Jesus for as long as I could remember, but I had never written down how God was working in my life or what I was learning.

Because of Linda's encouragement, I purchased a basic journal to start writing down Bible verses, sermon notes, and the details of my everyday life. I had no rhyme or reason to what I wrote at first, but it felt so good to write what I was learning and feeling.

Unexpectedly, one month after I began journaling, I was diagnosed with breast cancer. Though the news was devastating, I now had a front row seat to see God and His glory and planned to record my journey using the journaling habits I already had put in place just a month before.

God is so good!

I can tell you from my experience that there is power in writing His Word on paper. If you record what He shows you using the 7 step method, you will be able to clearly see His hand in your life. You will be able to learn and record the truths and promises that He has for you.

Today, I am cancer free, but during my difficult cancer journey, I was able to experience peace and love from God that I had never experienced before. I also now have journals with written words that remind me of God's truths and my past experiences that one day my children and grandchildren can read when I'm no longer here. They will see a legacy of faith I hope to leave behind.

I want this for you too, so let's get started!

Here's how to use this guided journal

What you hold in your hands is a guided-journal using a method that God has put on my heart after many powerful journaling experiences. I am proof that if God puts something on your heart and you step out in faith and obedience, He will be faithful to use it for His good. I have asked the Lord to use me and speak through me to do great things for His Kingdom. My mission is to help others fall in love with God and His Word, and I know this book will help you to do just that!

The 7 steps will help you to seek after God and easily learn what He is saying to you, personally.

You may be saying to yourself, "What supplies or tools would be best for journaling through God's Word?"

First of all you do not have to buy any special items! You can keep things simple while focusing on learning more about Jesus and His Word. But if you do want to play around creatively, here is a basic list of my favorite journaling tools: www.AngellaBundz.com/tools

Understanding the 7 Steps

1. Scripture

After finding which topic you would like to study, you will start by looking up the verse that is listed on the top of the page. You can use whatever Bible translation that you prefer. Some Bible translations are more literal and others are more of a paraphrase. You also can use a Bible app on your phone if you prefer. Personally, I like to hold the Word on paper in my hands.

Next, you will write down the verse in your own handwriting. There are benefits to actually writing Scripture. It helps you to slow down, lean in, and really read the words. It also helps you to interact with His words and not be a passive observer. You can see the details that you may have missed if you were reading too quickly.

Looking up the Scripture ourselves helps us become more familiar with our Bible. There truly is power in the Word when it is written on paper. Don't worry...you don't need to be an artist or have beautiful handwriting to do this step. Simply write the verse to get it into your head and heart. If you do want to bring more artistry to the process, feel free to unleash your creativity! (I even have some blank pages in the book for this purpose.

2. Soak It In

Next, you will read a verse or verses a few times—even aloud. The repetitive reading of the same verse will help your spirit to soak in the message God has for you.

TIP: You may want to read different versions of the Bible to see if they make the verse easier to understand.

3. Search Meanings

This step is a favorite of many who use the 7-step method. You will write words and definitions of hard or new words that you come across in the Scripture reading. Sometimes even looking up a common word like "joy" will bring new understanding to the Scripture. When you understand the Word of God better, the verses really come alive in a personalized way.

4. Saying to Me

In this step, you will write down what you feel God is showing you about the verses you are studying. This will be a little different to everyone, because God wants a personal relationship with each of us. When we learn about God's truths and His love for us, it is very powerful to write down what God reveals. You may not fully understand it now, but you may look back on it later and see God's hand moving! This is so powerful because it is not just a broad application; you are asking God to show you what He has for you, personally.

5. Set Your Mind

We are called in Colossians 3:2 to set our minds on things above, not on earthly things. So this is the step where you decide to set your mind and thoughts on the truths that you have learned. Although we cannot escape the stress and troubles of this world, we can choose to focus above on the truth and love of Jesus Christ. We *can* choose to believe the truths of God, not the lies and discouragements of the enemy. In this section, review what you have learned from the Bible verse(s) and write down a sentence or two that you choose to remember and carry with you.

6. Share

This is the step where you think about ways you can share the truths you have learned with others. You can do this through a number of ways such as sharing a social media post, sending a text to a family member, setting up a coffee date with a friend, or by mailing a note that shares what you've learned with a loved one. Wearing a necklace with Scripture on it is another way to share with others what you have learned about God and His Word. You could even hang a Scripture verse in your home for others to see!

7. Say It In A Prayer

In this last step, you will write a simple prayer to God. He loves spending time with you. Remember, prayer is just talking and listening to God. It helps us form a closer relationship with Him. There are many Bible verses with promises that talk about prayer. These prayers in this step are generally related to the Bible topic you are studying. You will then have a record of prayers that you can go back and read again and again. It is an honor to be able to talk to God at any time about anything.

Those are the 7 steps that you will repeat each and every day. Along the way, you will gain a new understanding of God's Word that brings meaning and life to you. Draw near to Him and develop a habit of seeking His will for your life!

On the next page you'll see a brief layout of the 7 steps to refer back to if you feel stuck along the way.

Remember, there is no perfection here. Jesus Christ is the only perfect one who ever lived. Our goal here is to fall in love with God and His Word. If you feel stuck or unsure, you can literally say to God, "Lord, I am not understanding this, please help me." We can ask the Holy Spirit to reveal His truths. He is here for you, and I am too.

I can't wait for you to get started!

Angella

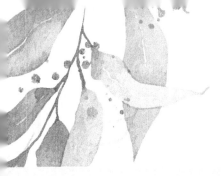

7 SIMPLE STEPS to STUDYING SCRIPTURE

1. SCRIPTURE—Write down the verse in your own handwriting.

2. SOAK IT IN—Meditate on the Word by reading the verse at least three times and even saying it out loud.

3. SEARCH MEANINGS—Write down the word(s) that you don't understand or want to learn about, and search their meanings.

4. SAYING TO ME—Write down what you feel God is showing you through that verse.

5. SET YOUR MIND—Write down what you choose to carry with you and keep in your thoughts.

6. SHARE—Plan how you will share what you've learned.

7. SAY IT IN A PRAYER—Pray a simple prayer to God.

Sample Journal Entry

Date: 6/30/20

Psalm 36:7

1 Scripture "How priceless is your unfailing love, O God. People take refuge in the shadow of your wings."

2 Soak It In reread and read outloud.

3 Search Meanings priceless - a value beyond all price, invaluable

unfailing - endless, completely dependable

refuge - place of shelter, protection from danger or trouble

shadow - shade

4 *Saying To Me* — Your love for me, God, is endless! Your love is completely dependable! It is beyond any price. I rest in you as a place of shelter. You are trustworthy Lord.

5 *Set Your Mind* — I choose to remember that your love for me endless and does not fail me. I can take refuge in you.

6 *Share* — I shared this verse Friday on my social media accounts.

7 *Say It In a Prayer*

Dear Heavenly Father,
Thank you for your love for me that is priceless and never ends. I am so grateful that I can take refuge in you. I love you Lord. Please help me to show and share this love with others.
In Jesus' Precious name, Amen

My prayer for you...

God wants you to know Him and His love for you! His Word was given to us with love, grace, and truth.

> Dear Lord, I pray for each woman who is reading this journal. I ask that she fall in love with you and your Word in a new and meaningful way. I ask you, Holy Spirit, to please give her clarity and understanding as she studies her Bible. I also pray that she will experience how wide and long and high and deep Your love is for her. I pray that this book isn't the end, but the beginning of her journey seeking after You with all of her heart. We pray this knowing that you are able to do immeasurably more than we ask or imagine, according to Your power that is at work within us. We thank you Lord. Amen.

I cannot wait to hear about all God will do in and through you through *7 Simple Steps*, my friend.

Table of Contents

God's Love For You

Psalm 36:7 2
Psalm 86:15 4
Psalm 143:8 6
Psalm 145:8-9 8
Isaiah 54:10 10
Lamentations 3:22-24 12
Zephaniah 3:17 14
Romans 5:8 16
Romans 8:38-39 18
1 John 4:9-11 20

Seeking After God

Deuteronomy 4:29 26
1 Chronicles 16:11-12 28
Psalm 9:10 30
Psalm 34:10 32
Psalm 63:1 34
Psalm 105:4 36
Psalm 119:2 38
Jeremiah 29:13 40

When You Feel Afraid

Deuteronomy 31:6 46
Psalm 56:3 48
Isaiah 41:13 50
Isaiah 43:1-2 52
Isaiah 43:5 54
John 14:27 56
1 Peter 5:7 58

Put Your Hope In The Lord

Psalm 43:5 64
Psalm 71:5 66
Psalm 119:147 68
Psalm 130:5-7 70
Romans 15:13 72

God's Word

2 Samuel 22:31 78
Psalm 18:30 80
Psalm 119:105 82
Psalm 119:130 84
Proverbs 4:5 86
Isaiah 40:8 88
Colossians 3:16 90

Thanking God

1 Chronicles 16:34 96
1 Chronicles 29:13 98
Psalm 9:1 100
Psalm 28:7 102
Psalm 95:2-3 104
Psalm 106:1 106
1 Thessalonians 5:16-18 108

Strength Through Trials

Joshua 1:9	114
Psalm 46:1-3	116
Psalm 73:26	118
Isaiah 40:29	120
Isaiah 41:10	122
Jeremiah 32:17	124
Luke 18:27	126
Ephesians 3:20-21	128
Phillippians 4:13	130
2 Thessalonians 3:3	132

Waiting On God

Psalm 27:14	138
Psalm 130:5	140
Isaiah 55:8	142
Lamentations 3:25	144
Micah 7:7	146
Luke 18:27	148

When You Feel Sad

Psalm 3:3	154
Psalm 5:2	156
Psalm 34:18	158
Psalm 37:39	160
Psalm 40:1-2	162
Matthew 11:28	164

Praise The Lord

1 Chronicles 16:34	170
Psalm 9:1	172
Psalm 63:3-4	174
Psalm 104:33	176
Psalm 105:1	178
Psalm 145:3	180
Isaiah 25:1	182

Who God Says You Are

Isaiah 43:1	188
John 1:12	190
Romans 3:24	192
Romans 8:1	194
Romans 8:37	196
2 Corinthians 5:17	198
Ephesians 1:3	200

Believing In A Savior

John 3:16	206
John 6:47	208
John 20:31	210
Romans 10:9	212
Galatians 2:20	214
Ephesians 1:7	216

GOD'S LOVE FOR YOU

God's Love for You

Date: _____

Psalm 36:7

1 Scripture

2 Soak It In

3 Search Meanings

4 Saying To Me

5 Set Your Mind

6 Share

7 Say It In a Prayer

God's Love for You

Date: _____

Psalm 86:15

1 Scripture

2 Soak It In

3 Search Meanings

4 Saying To Me

5 Set Your Mind

6 Share

7 Say It In a Prayer

God's Love for You

Date: _____

Psalm 143:8

1 Scripture

_____
_____
_____
_____
_____

2 Soak It In

_____
_____
_____

3 Search Meanings

_____
_____
_____
_____
_____
_____
_____

4   Saying To Me

5   Set Your Mind

6   Share

7   Say It In a Prayer

God's Love for You

Date: _____

Psalm 145:8-9

1 Scripture

2 Soak It In

3 Search Meanings

4 Saying To Me

5 Set Your Mind

6 Share

7 Say It In a Prayer

God's Love for You

Date:

Isaiah 54:10

1 Scripture

2 Soak It In

3 Search Meanings

4 Saying To Me

5 Set Your Mind

6 Share

7 Say It In a Prayer

God's Love for You

Date:

Lamentations 3:22-24

1 Scripture

2 Soak It In

3 Search Meanings

4   Saying To Me

5   Set Your Mind

6   Share

7   Say It In a Prayer

God's Love for You

Date: _____

Zephaniah 3:17

1 Scripture

2 Soak It In

3 Search Meanings

4 Saying To Me

5 Set Your Mind

6 Share

7 Say It In a Prayer

God's Love for You

Date:

Romans 5:8

1 Scripture

2 Soak It In

3 Search Meanings

4 Saying To Me

5 Set Your Mind

6 Share

7 Say It In a Prayer

God's Love for You

Date: _____

Romans 8:38-39

1 Scripture

2 Soak It In

3 Search Meanings

4   Saying To Me

5   Set Your Mind

6   Share

7   Say It In a Prayer

God's Love for You

Date: _____

1 John 4:9-11

1 Scripture

2 Soak It In

3 Search Meanings

4 Saying To Me

5 Set Your Mind

6 Share

7 Say It In a Prayer

SEEKING AFTER GOD

Seeking After God

Date: _____

Deuteronomy 4:29

1 Scripture

2 Soak It In

3 Search Meanings

4 Saying To Me

5 Set Your Mind

6 Share

7 Say It In a Prayer

Seeking After God

Date: _____

1 Chronicles 16:11-12

1 Scripture

2 Soak It In

3 Search Meanings

4 Saying To Me

5 Set Your Mind

6 Share

7 Say It In a Prayer

Seeking After God

Date: _____

Psalm 9:10

1 Scripture

2 Soak It In

3 Search Meanings

4 Saying To Me

5 Set Your Mind

6 Share

7 Say It In a Prayer

Seeking After God

Date:

Psalm 34:10

1 Scripture

2 Soak It In

3 Search Meanings

4   Saying To Me

5   Set Your Mind

6   Share

7   Say It In a Prayer

Seeking After God

Date:

Psalm 63:1

1 Scripture

2 Soak It In

3 Search Meanings

4 Saying To Me

5 Set Your Mind

6 Share

7 Say It In a Prayer

Seeking After God

Date: _____

Psalm 105:4

1 Scripture

2 Soak It In

3 Search Meanings

4 Saying To Me

5 Set Your Mind

6 Share

7 Say It In a Prayer

Seeking After God

Date: _____

Psalm 119:2

1 Scripture

2 Soak It In

3 Search Meanings

4 Saying To Me

5 Set Your Mind

6 Share

7 Say It In a Prayer

Seeking After God

Date: _____

Jeremiah 29:13

1 Scripture

2 Soak It In

3 Search Meanings

4 Saying To Me

5 Set Your Mind

6 Share

7 Say It In a Prayer

WHEN YOU FEEL AFRAID

When You Feel Afraid

Date: _____

Deuteronomy 31:6

1 Scripture

2 Soak It In

3 Search Meanings

4 Saying To Me

5 Set Your Mind

6 Share

7 Say It In a Prayer

When You Feel Afraid

Date: _____

Psalm 56:3

1 Scripture

2 Soak It In

3 Search Meanings

4   Saying To Me

5   Set Your Mind

6   Share

7   Say It In a Prayer

When You Feel Afraid

Date: _____

Isaiah 41:13

1 Scripture

2 Soak It In

3 Search Meanings

4 Saying To Me

5 Set Your Mind

6 Share

7 Say It In a Prayer

When You Feel Afraid

Date: _____

Isaiah 43:1-2

1 Scripture

2 Soak It In

3 Search Meanings

4   Saying To Me

5   Set Your Mind

6   Share

7   Say It In a Prayer

When You Feel Afraid

Date: _____

Isaiah 43:5

1 Scripture

2 Soak It In

3 Search Meanings

4 Saying To Me

5 Set Your Mind

6 Share

7 Say It In a Prayer

When You Feel Afraid

Date: _____

John 14:27

1 Scripture

2 Soak It In

3 Search Meanings

4   Saying To Me

5   Set Your Mind

6   Share

7   Say It In a Prayer

When You Feel Afraid

Date: _____

1 Peter 5:7

1 Scripture

2 Soak It In

3 Search Meanings

4   Saying To Me

5   Set Your Mind

6   Share

7   Say It In a Prayer

PUT YOUR HOPE IN THE LORD

Put Your Hope in the Lord

Date: _____

Psalm 43:5

1 Scripture

2 Soak It In

3 Search Meanings

4 Saying To Me

5 Set Your Mind

6 Share

7 Say It In a Prayer

Put Your Hope in the Lord

Date: _____

Psalm 71:5

1 Scripture

2 Soak It In

3 Search Meanings

4   Saying To Me

5   Set Your Mind

6   Share

7   Say It In a Prayer

Put Your Hope in the Lord

Date: _____

Psalm 119:147

1 Scripture

2 Soak It In

3 Search Meanings

4 Saying To Me

5 Set Your Mind

6 Share

7 Say It In a Prayer

Put Your Hope in the Lord

Date: _____

Psalm 130:5-7

1 Scripture

2 Soak It In

3 Search Meanings

4   Saying To Me

5   Set Your Mind

6   Share

7   Say It In a Prayer

Put Your Hope in the Lord

Date: _____

Romans 15:13

1 Scripture

2 Soak It In

3 Search Meanings

4 Saying To Me

5 Set Your Mind

6 Share

7 Say It In a Prayer

GOD'S WORD

God's Word

Date: _____

2 Samuel 22:31

1 Scripture

2 Soak It In

3 Search Meanings

4 Saying To Me

5 Set Your Mind

6 Share

7 Say It In a Prayer

God's Word

Date: _____

Psalm 18:30

1 Scripture

2 Soak It In

3 Search Meanings

4 Saying To Me

5 Set Your Mind

6 Share

7 Say It In a Prayer

God's Word

Date: _____

Psalm 119:105

1 Scripture

2 Soak It In

3 Search Meanings

4 Saying To Me

5 Set Your Mind

6 Share

7 Say It In a Prayer

God's Word

Date: _____

Psalm 119:130

1 Scripture

2 Soak It In

3 Search Meanings

4　Saying To Me

5　Set Your Mind

6　Share

7　Say It In a Prayer

God's Word

Date: _____

Proverbs 4:5

1 Scripture

2 Soak It In

3 Search Meanings

4   Saying To Me

5   Set Your Mind

6   Share

7   Say It In a Prayer

God's Word

Date: _____

Isaiah 40:8

1 Scripture

2 Soak It In

3 Search Meanings

4 Saying To Me

5 Set Your Mind

6 Share

7 Say It In a Prayer

God's Word

Date: _____

Colossians 3:16

1 Scripture

2 Soak It In

3 Search Meanings

4 Saying To Me

5 Set Your Mind

6 Share

7 Say It In a Prayer

THANKING GOD

Thanking God

Date: _____

1 Chronicles 16:34

1 Scripture

2 Soak It In

3 Search Meanings

4   Saying To Me

5   Set Your Mind

6   Share

7   Say It In a Prayer

Thanking God

Date: _____

1 Chronicles 29:13

1 Scripture

2 Soak It In

3 Search Meanings

4   Saying To Me

5   Set Your Mind

6   Share

7   Say It In a Prayer

Thanking God

Date: _____

Psalm 9:1

1 Scripture

2 Soak It In

3 Search Meanings

4 Saying To Me

5 Set Your Mind

6 Share

7 Say It In a Prayer

Thanking God

Date: _____

Psalm 28:7

1 Scripture

2 Soak It In

3 Search Meanings

4 Saying To Me

5 Set Your Mind

6 Share

7 Say It In a Prayer

Thanking God

Date: _____

Psalm 95:2-3

1 Scripture

2 Soak It In

3 Search Meanings

4   Saying To Me

5   Set Your Mind

6   Share

7   Say It In a Prayer

Thanking God

Date:

Psalm 106:1

1 Scripture

2 Soak It In

3 Search Meanings

4 Saying To Me

5 Set Your Mind

6 Share

7 Say It In a Prayer

Thanking God

Date: _____

1 Thessalonians 5:16-18

1 Scripture

2 Soak It In

3 Search Meanings

4 Saying To Me

5 Set Your Mind

6 Share

7 Say It In a Prayer

iii

STRENGTH THROUGH TRIALS

Strength Through Trials

Date:

Joshua 1:9

1 Scripture

2 Soak It In

3 Search Meanings

4 Saying To Me

5 Set Your Mind

6 Share

7 Say It In a Prayer

Strength Through Trials

Date:

Psalm 46:1-3

1 Scripture

2 Soak It In

3 Search Meanings

4 Saying To Me

5 Set Your Mind

6 Share

7 Say It In a Prayer

Strength Through Trials

Date:

Psalm 73:26

1 Scripture

2 Soak It In

3 Search Meanings

4   Saying To Me

5   Set Your Mind

6   Share

7   Say It In a Prayer

Strength Through Trials

Date: _____

Isaiah 40:29

1 Scripture

2 Soak It In

3 Search Meanings

4 Saying To Me

5 Set Your Mind

6 Share

7 Say It In a Prayer

Strength Through Trials

Date: _____

Isaiah 41:10

1 Scripture

_____

2 Soak It In

_____

3 Search Meanings

_____

4 Saying To Me

5 Set Your Mind

6 Share

7 Say It In a Prayer

Strength Through Trials

Date: _____

Jeremiah 32:17

1 Scripture

2 Soak It In

3 Search Meanings

4 Saying To Me

5 Set Your Mind

6 Share

7 Say It In a Prayer

Strength Through Trials

Date:

Luke 18:27

1 Scripture

2 Soak It In

3 Search Meanings

4 Saying To Me

5 Set Your Mind

6 Share

7 Say It In a Prayer

Strength Through Trials

Date:

Ephesians 3:20-21

1 Scripture

2 Soak It In

3 Search Meanings

4 Saying To Me

5 Set Your Mind

6 Share

7 Say It In a Prayer

Strength Through Trials

Date: _____

Philippians 4:13

1 Scripture

2 Soak It In

3 Search Meanings

4 Saying To Me

5 Set Your Mind

6 Share

7 Say It In a Prayer

Strength Through Trials

Date: _____

2 Thessalonians 3:3

1 Scripture

2 Soak It In

3 Search Meanings

4 Saying To Me

5 Set Your Mind

6 Share

7 Say It In a Prayer

WAITING ON GOD

Waiting on God

Date: _____

Psalm 27:14

1 Scripture

2 Soak It In

3 Search Meanings

4　Saying To Me

5　Set Your Mind

6　Share

7　Say It In a Prayer

Waiting on God

Date: _____

Psalm 130:5

1 Scripture

2 Soak It In

3 Search Meanings

4 Saying To Me

5 Set Your Mind

6 Share

7 Say It In a Prayer

Waiting on God

Date: _____

Isaiah 55:8

1 Scripture

2 Soak It In

3 Search Meanings

4   Saying To Me

5   Set Your Mind

6   Share

7   Say It In a Prayer

Waiting on God

Date: _____

Lamentations 3:25

1 Scripture

2 Soak It In

3 Search Meanings

4 Saying To Me

5 Set Your Mind

6 Share

7 Say It In a Prayer

Waiting on God

Date: _____

Micah 7:7

1 Scripture

2 Soak It In

3 Search Meanings

4 Saying To Me

5 Set Your Mind

6 Share

7 Say It In a Prayer

Waiting on God

Date: _____

Luke 18:27

1 Scripture

2 Soak It In

3 Search Meanings

4   Saying To Me

5   Set Your Mind

6   Share

7   Say It In a Prayer

WHEN YOU FEEL SAD

When You Feel Sad

Date:

Psalm 3:3

1 Scripture

2 Soak It In

3 Search Meanings

4 Saying To Me

5 Set Your Mind

6 Share

7 Say It In a Prayer

When You Feel Sad

Date: _____

Psalm 5:2

1 Scripture

2 Soak It In

3 Search Meanings

4 Saying To Me

5 Set Your Mind

6 Share

7 Say It In a Prayer

When You Feel Sad

Date: _____

Psalm 34:18

1 Scripture

2 Soak It In

3 Search Meanings

4   Saying To Me

5   Set Your Mind

6   Share

7   Say It In a Prayer

When You Feel Sad

Date: _____

Psalm 37:39

1 Scripture

2 Soak It In

3 Search Meanings

4 Saying To Me

5 Set Your Mind

6 Share

7 Say It In a Prayer

When You Feel Sad

Date: _____

Psalm 40:1-2

1 Scripture

2 Soak It In

3 Search Meanings

4 Saying To Me

5 Set Your Mind

6 Share

7 Say It In a Prayer

When You Feel Sad

Date: _____

Matthew 11:28

1 Scripture

2 Soak It In

3 Search Meanings

4 Saying To Me

5 Set Your Mind

6 Share

7 Say It In a Prayer

PRAISE THE LORD

Praise the Lord

Date: _____

1 Chronicles 16:34

1 Scripture

2 Soak It In

3 Search Meanings

4 Saying To Me

5 Set Your Mind

6 Share

7 Say It In a Prayer

Praise the Lord

Date: _____

Psalm 9:1

1 Scripture

2 Soak It In

3 Search Meanings

4   Saying To Me

5   Set Your Mind

6   Share

7   Say It In a Prayer

Praise the Lord

Date: _____

Psalm 63:3-4

1 Scripture

2 Soak It In

3 Search Meanings

4 Saying To Me

5 Set Your Mind

6 Share

7 Say It In a Prayer

Praise the Lord

Date: _____

Psalm 104:33

1 Scripture

2 Soak It In

3 Search Meanings

4 Saying To Me

5 Set Your Mind

6 Share

7 Say It In a Prayer

Praise the Lord

Date: _____

Psalm 105:1

1 Scripture

2 Soak It In

3 Search Meanings

4   Saying To Me

5   Set Your Mind

6   Share

7   Say It In a Prayer

Praise the Lord

Date:

Psalm 145:3

1 Scripture

2 Soak It In

3 Search Meanings

4 Saying To Me

5 Set Your Mind

6 Share

7 Say It In a Prayer

Praise the Lord

Date:

Isaiah 25:1

1 Scripture

2 Soak It In

3 Search Meanings

4 Saying To Me

5 Set Your Mind

6 Share

7 Say It In a Prayer

WHO GOD SAYS YOU ARE

Who God Says You Are

Date: _____

Isaiah 43:1

1 Scripture

_____
_____
_____
_____

2 Soak It In

_____
_____
_____

3 Search Meanings

_____
_____
_____
_____
_____
_____
_____

4   Saying To Me

5   Set Your Mind

6   Share

7   Say It In a Prayer

Who God Says You Are

Date: _____

John 1:12

1 Scripture

2 Soak It In

3 Search Meanings

4 Saying To Me

5 Set Your Mind

6 Share

7 Say It In a Prayer

Who God Says You Are

Date: _____

Romans 3:24

1 Scripture

2 Soak It In

3 Search Meanings

4 Saying To Me

5 Set Your Mind

6 Share

7 Say It In a Prayer

Who God Says You Are

Date: _____

Romans 8:1

1 Scripture

2 Soak It In

3 Search Meanings

4 Saying To Me

5 Set Your Mind

6 Share

7 Say It In a Prayer

Who God Says You Are

Date: _____

Romans 8:37

1 Scripture

2 Soak It In

3 Search Meanings

4 Saying To Me

5 Set Your Mind

6 Share

7 Say It In a Prayer

Who God Says You Are

Date: _____

2 Corinthians 5:17

1 Scripture

2 Soak It In

3 Search Meanings

4   Saying To Me

5   Set Your Mind

6   Share

7   Say It In a Prayer

Who God Says You Are

Date: _____

Ephesians 1:3

1 Scripture

2 Soak It In

3 Search Meanings

4 Saying To Me

5 Set Your Mind

6 Share

7 Say It In a Prayer

BELIEVING IN A SAVIOR

Believing in a Savior

Date:

John 3:16

1 Scripture

2 Soak It In

3 Search Meanings

4   Saying To Me

5   Set Your Mind

6   Share

7   Say It In a Prayer

Believing in a Savior

Date: _____

John 6:47

1 Scripture

2 Soak It In

3 Search Meanings

4 Saying To Me

5 Set Your Mind

6 Share

7 Say It In a Prayer

Believing in a Savior

Date: _____

John 20:31

1 Scripture

2 Soak It In

3 Search Meanings

4 Saying To Me

5 Set Your Mind

6 Share

7 Say It In a Prayer

Believing in a Savior

Date:

Romans 10:9

1 Scripture

2 Soak It In

3 Search Meanings

4   Saying To Me

5   Set Your Mind

6   Share

7   Say It In a Prayer

Believing in a Savior

Date:

Galatians 2:20

1 Scripture

2 Soak It In

3 Search Meanings

4 Saying To Me

5 Set Your Mind

6 Share

7 Say It In a Prayer

Believing in a Savior

Date: _____

Ephesians 1:7

1 Scripture

2 Soak It In

3 Search Meanings

4   Saying To Me

5   Set Your Mind

6   Share

7   Say It In a Prayer

Made in the USA
Middletown, DE
11 August 2020